P9-CDE-741

DISCARD

sibling rivalry

SIBLING RIVALRY

brothers and sisters at odds

BY ELAINE LANDAU

*illustrated by
Anne Canevari Green*

*The Millbrook Press
Brookfield, Connecticut*

Library of Congress Cataloging-in-Publication Data
Landau, Elaine.
Sibling rivalry : brothers and sisters at odds / by Elaine Landau.
p.   cm.
Includes bibliographical references and index.
Summary: Explores sibling rivalry through interviews and first-hand accounts, examining its causes, manifestations, and cures.
ISBN 1-56294-328-6 (lib. bdg.)
1. Sibling rivalry—Juvenile literature.   2. Sibling rivalry—Case studies—Juvenile literature.   3. Brothers and sisters—Juvenile literature.   4. Brothers and sisters—Case studies—Juvenile literature.   [1. Sibling rivalry.   2. Brothers and sisters.]
I. Title.
BF723.S43L36   1994
306.875—dc20   93-1262   CIP   AC

Published by The Millbrook Press
2 Old New Milford Road
Brookfield, Connecticut 06804

contents

Chapter One
  Second Best 9

Chapter Two
  What Makes Siblings Rivals? 14

Chapter Three
  Parents, Comparisons, and Competitors 25

Chapter Four
  Once Rivals, Always Rivals? 33

  Endnotes 43
  Further Reading 45
  Index 47

sibling rivalry

For older children, the struggle for parents' attention and affection can begin when a new baby enters the house—and the feeling of being Mom and Dad's only pride and joy goes out the window.

one

SECOND BEST

Beth speaks:

"It was never easy being Melanie's little sister. But it was *supposed* to be wonderful; our parents planned it that way. When we were small our mother used to tell everyone that she and my dad had us three years apart on purpose. She had read that spacing children that way was best. Melanie was supposed to be ready by then. She would be out of diapers, drinking from a glass, and not need our mother for everything. Mom was sure that Melanie would welcome the love and fun a little brother or sister would bring. Yeah, right!

"My sister wasn't at all thrilled with my arrival. I remember our parents describing how Melanie would grab my bottle or a toy from my crib and run through the house with it. The louder I screamed, the tighter she clung to it. But after a while, Melanie calmed down and felt better about me.

— *9*

"Bravo for Melanie, but what about me? When there's a new baby, everyone worries about how the older child feels. It isn't fair. Being born second can make you feel second best. There are stacks of photo albums and videos of my sister. Mom started an album for me, but there weren't enough snapshots to fill it. It has mostly pictures of Melanie and me together or the two of us with our parents or grandparents.

"Being younger meant that I felt like I missed out on lots of things. Every morning I watched my mother help Melanie get ready for school. She always had pretty things to wear, a great lunch box, and a pencil set with colored pencils. I used to cry when the school bus left without me. Melanie said I couldn't go because I was a baby. Melanie could be real mean.

"I was also too young for the special treats Melanie enjoyed. We lived just outside of New York City and when the Ringling Brothers and Barnum and Bailey Circus—"The Greatest Show on Earth"— came to town, our aunt Karen offered to take my sister. They would stay at a hotel, eat in restaurants, and see the show. I couldn't go because I was too little to be away from home.

"Melanie came back thrilled. Aunt Karen bought her a bunch of stuff at the circus. My favorite was a little monkey in a red hat and jacket that danced from a stick. But when I tried to play with it, Melanie snatched it away. My mother told me not to touch it and that she would buy something for me the next day. She came home with a green plastic turtle that you pulled along the floor with a string. It wasn't furry and it didn't have great clothes like the monkey. When I asked Melanie if she wanted to trade, she laughed at me. I never got to play with the monkey until it was really old and Melanie was tired of it. I didn't want it either then. The monkey's clothes were gone, its head was bent back, and it didn't dance anymore.

Jealousy and competitiveness between brothers and sisters can happen when younger children feel that because they came second, they were left out of the spotlight.

"More than anything, I wanted to be Melanie's age. Yet I knew that no matter how much I grew, my sister would still be older. It didn't seem right. Melanie was always going to be first, while I was the one left behind. And I can't understand why our parents were so concerned about how Melanie would feel about having a little sister."

— *11*

Beth's feelings about Melanie are not uncommon. In fact, it's rare to grow up with brothers and sisters and not experience even a twinge of what both Beth and Melanie felt at times toward one another. Such feelings are the result of sibling rivalry, a term used to describe the jealousy and competitiveness that can exist between brothers and sisters.

Sibling rivalry can occur not only when children like Beth feel "second best" compared to their older brothers and sisters. Children like Melanie can also feel "second best." A new baby's arrival can be difficult for older children. They can be upset over having to share their parents' love and attention with infants. Sharon Farber, a psychotherapist—a person who helps people work out emotional problems—explains why:

> *Although most of us don't admit it very readily, all of us wish to be loved exclusively by our parents. . . . The first-born is often able to maintain the fantasy that he or she is the mother's only love until the second child comes along. Then that dose of reality [of not being the only one parents love] is experienced quite brutally.*[1]

Whether it's the result of brothers and sisters feeling left out or less loved because of each other, sibling rivalry can cause problems. These problems can range from normal everyday scrapes to serious emotional, and even physical, illnesses.

If you think sibling rivalry is only for kids, moreover, think again. While adults aren't likely to snatch their brothers' or sisters' possessions for spite, they can express jealousy and competitiveness in less obvious but important ways.

In this book, we'll investigate sibling rivalry. We'll look at the factors that influence it and at its effects. We'll also consider what can be done about it. Throughout this book we'll present the stories of real people, some of whose names have been changed, like Beth's. They have all experienced this common occurrence firsthand. Some of them might remind you of people you know, and you may even recognize in them a little bit of you.

two

WHAT MAKES SIBLINGS RIVALS?

Many factors influence how siblings feel about one another. These factors can also affect the degree to which brothers and sisters experience sibling rivalry. Here are some of the major factors:

Contact

The amount of contact brothers and sisters have helps to determine how they feel about each other. Siblings born ten or more years apart generally have the least contact. Their age differences make it unlikely that they'll spend as much time together as brothers and sisters closer in age. While one sibling is off at college or living on his or her own, the younger brother or sister may just be entering second grade. These siblings will have different childhood friends and experiences. They may also never have to depend on each other's help in a difficult situation. As a result, such brothers and sisters, though they love each other, tend to be emotionally less close.

This emotional distance discourages sibling rivalry. Age differences between such brothers and sisters make it unlikely that they will feel strongly enough about the same things to be competitive. A sixteen-year-old isn't likely to feel jealous when her parents praise her six-year-old brother for learning how to read. Chances are the six-year-old won't feel cheated when the parents allow his sister to borrow the family car as a reward for doing well on her chemistry exam.

Siblings who are closer in age tend to be emotionally much closer. Often these brothers or sisters have shared a bedroom, had the same teachers, and worn the same hand-me-down clothes. They may also have had the same circle of friends, played on some of the same sports teams, and taken part together in church or synagogue youth activities.

These siblings are usually best able to stir in one another not only a great deal of affection but competitiveness as well. One seventeen-year-old boy described how his brothers, both close to his age, affected him:

"I had to do well in class. I didn't have a choice. Not getting good grades was out of the question for a kid with two brilliant older brothers. Mark, the oldest, was three years older than I. But I was just eleven months younger than Eric [the middle brother]. We looked so much alike that sometimes people thought we were twins. And I was not about to let anyone think Eric was the smart 'twin' and I was the dumb one."

Rivalry divided the brothers, but it inspired a healthy sense of competition that actually brought the boys together as well. The seventeen-year-old continued:

"Mark taught Eric and me how to play chess. The two of us took turns playing against him most weekends, and all of us really looked forward to those matches. Our parents even enjoyed watching us play.

"At first Mark let us win a lot. But after a while we improved, and once Eric started beating him, Mark began making excuses for not playing anymore. He would say that he had something else to do or someplace to go, but he didn't look that busy. Even though he loved chess, I guess he hated being beaten by his little brother more."

Family Size

Family size frequently influences sibling relationships. In the late 1800s and early 1900s, it was not unusual for a young person to have four or five brothers and sisters. While many of these siblings were close in age and tended to be emotionally close, they may have experienced less rivalry.

This was especially true for the waves of immigrant families arriving on America's shores as the country grew. The children in these families tended to be protective of one another. Having to adjust to a new language and culture was difficult to do alone. Siblings tended to bond together. They took comfort in having others close in age who came from the same homeland and shared many of the same memories. Sibling support in these families often outweighed sibling rivalry.

Through the years, however, American families have gotten smaller. This has been due to, among other things, financial concerns—the cost of having children has risen—as well as increased family planning. More women have careers and work outside the home. According to some, this has prompted women to choose more carefully when they will have children and to have fewer children.

— *16*

As a result, the average young person in the United States today is usually part of a two-child family. He or she grows up with only one brother or sister. When a child has only a single sibling, the bond between them is often more intense than when there are others. Instead of having a few young people around to cheer each other up when things go wrong or to share family fun times, the two siblings depend on just one another for support.

Because of this, sibling rivalry can also be intense. As circumstances change and one sibling goes off to school or sleep-away camp, the one left behind may feel jealous or left out, or have a sense of emptiness in his or her life.

Direct comparisons by kids and parents are also more likely to be made. A child with obvious talents—one who excels at sports, for example—may appear "better" if his or her only sibling possesses talents that are slower to develop in childhood, such as artistic talents. In families with four or five children, on the other hand, it's less probable that a very talented child will make any single brother or sister look bad. The other children often display varying degrees of talent, making it less likely for one child to appear "better" and the others second best.

Competition for parents' love and attention is often keener in small families as well. When children in these families feel short-changed of their parents' affection, they have only one other person to blame for "stealing" it. In a larger family, however, children more readily accept that they'll have to share their mother and father. They have adjusted to this as their family has grown through the years. Often the older children turn into "little parents" themselves. They frequently baby-sit and take on more household chores. Their younger brothers and sisters become their responsibilities rather than their rivals.

Families with two children of the same sex tend to experience more sibling rivalry: Direct comparison between children is likely, and when one child feels left out there's only one other child to blame.

Gender

The gender, or sex, of a family's children also influences how siblings interact. Sharing many of the same life experiences, same-sex siblings tend to be most close. This is especially true of sisters—the siblings that experts claim have the strongest bond.[1] Since girls often tend to express their feelings more openly than boys, they may more readily form close emotional ties with each other. Some girls feel that no one knows them better or means more to them than their sister.

— *18*

Rivalry also tends to be stronger among siblings of the same sex. Because these brothers and sisters tend to have so much in common—in some cases they may even look alike—they often struggle against one another to stand out in their parents' eyes and in the eyes of others. We'll look at just how extreme this struggle can be in Chapter 3.

Physical differences and social stereotypes have discouraged rivalry between siblings of different sexes. Even if a brother and sister both enjoyed bodybuilding, for example, they would probably be judged in separate male and female categories.

This may be changing, however. A girl may no longer be told that she isn't expected to do as well as her brothers in math and science. With increasing numbers of women advancing in society, girls have been challenging boys for academic honors in traditionally male-dominated areas such as these. They may find themselves competing increasingly with their brothers.

Divorce and Stepfamilies

Marriages are supposed to last a lifetime, but they don't always. According to some estimates nearly forty out of every one hundred children born will be affected by divorce. A family's breakup (which can be caused by the death of a parent as well as divorce) can bring on a broad range of moods and emotions: Children may feel sadness, guilt, fear, or anger at different times.

The situation can affect sibling relationships as well. With one parent out of the home, the other parent can become more occupied doing chores previously shared with a husband or wife. Family roles frequently shift as a result. The "baby" may have to grow up more quickly, while older children often take on extra responsibility. At times, siblings may bond together. They may look to each other for comfort and security in the face of these changes.

In other instances, however, any existing rivalry among brothers and sisters can grow worse. This frequently happens if one child was the "favorite" of the parent who left the household. Feeling deprived of a special status, he or she may resent sharing attention from the remaining parent with brothers and sisters.

After divorces, many children have to adjust to either one or both of their parents remarrying. While these new families can be rewarding, they are rarely conflict-free, especially at the start. A child

When parents split up, children can find themselves isolated from both Mom and Dad and dependent on each other for comfort.

— 20

may spend a great deal of time with the divorced parent with whom he or she lives. If that parent remarries, it may be difficult to accept an "outsider"—a new spouse—who takes the parent's attention away as well as assumes a position of authority. If the new wife or husband brings children from a former marriage into the home, sibling rivalry may arise.

One twelve-year-old boy described his stepfamily experience as "the invasion of the possession snatchers":

"After the divorce, my two sisters stayed with my mom in our old house and I moved in with my dad. I wanted it that way. Dad and I were always close, and I didn't want to be left with a bunch of girls.

"For the first year or so things were great. I saw my mother twice a week and after a while I don't think I even minded the divorce that much. Dad and I were like roommates. We went to ball games, shot hoops together almost every evening, and did a lot of camping. We shared the cooking and housework too. Everybody said that we were like a couple of happy bachelors.

"Sometimes I missed my sisters, but then we would just plan to do something together. It was easier with them living at Mom's. I had a shot at getting into the bathroom every morning. I liked the way things were, but it didn't last. Before long Dad announced that he and his girlfriend, Margo, were getting married.

"I was never crazy about Margo to begin with. Maybe that's because Mom hated her so much. She said it wasn't fair for a woman to have three children and be that slim. But Dad made it clear that how I felt about Margo didn't matter. She'd be moving in with her furniture and her three brats.

"After the first week, I knew that my life would never be the same. We only had two kid bedrooms and now there were four of us. Margo had an older daughter and twin seven-year-old boys. Her daughter got her own room because she was a girl. I had to share the other room with the twins.

"My privacy was gone. Those two overran the place with stupid toys and Ninja Turtle gear. We were so crowded that Dad and Margo bought the twins bunk beds. I complained to my father about what was happening. He just told me to be glad that I wasn't in one of the bunks.

"Some of my friends thought the twins were cute, but they didn't live with them. The twins were miserable. One was whiny and a bed wetter. The other was a pint-sized bully. He always teased the bed wetter and made him cry.

"Margo said that they were still upset about her divorcing their father. That was supposed to be why they didn't sleep through the night. One would wake up the other, and then I'd be up too.

"But I think the worst thing was their claim on my father. The twins' father wasn't too good about visiting them. He would tell them that he was picking them up on Saturday and not show up. Then the bed wetter would cry and the bully would scream at him to shut up. Margo wanted my father to make it up to them by spending more time with her boys. Dad did what she asked. I felt bad because it was plain that he really enjoyed it.

"Dad and I didn't go camping by ourselves anymore. The bed wetter and bully always came along. There was hardly any time to shoot hoops either. Dad usually had to teach the twins something—like riding a two-wheeler or hitting and catching a ball. Dad and I are naturally athletic, but the twins were another story. I was amazed that they wanted to go out for Little League when they were so bad.

"Unfortunately, their dreams were always at my expense. My father spent every weekend working with them, which left almost no time for me. All of a sudden I wasn't supposed to need my father

ISN'T IT WONDERFUL HOW TWO STEPBROTHERS CAN PLAY TOGETHER SO QUIETLY?

When parents remarry, children can find themselves having to deal with a whole new set of family ties. Rivalry between stepbrothers and stepsisters can be especially intense.

anymore. Margo wanted me to help the twins as well. She didn't understand why I didn't feel sorry for two little boys without a father. But now they had a new father, and I hated that he was mine."

What if new siblings are born as a result of a new marriage of a divorced parent? New sets of grandparents can play important roles in these so-called "blended" families. When they take only their natural grandchildren on special trips or buy them lavish birthday presents, other children in the household may become envious.

Financial problems often loom large in these situations as well. With more people forced to live on the same amount of money, conflicts develop. At times a child may feel that he has less because of his half brother, half sister, or stepsibling.

Until the parents and children are able to work things out, the household may not be calm. A young person can easily resent new siblings for intruding on his or her "space" and perhaps even referring to a parent as "Mom" or "Dad." As tensions heighten, it's not uncommon to hear such phrases as "Get out of *my* room" or "He's not *your* father" echo through the halls of blended family homes.

three

PARENTS, COMPARISONS, AND COMPETITORS

Parents play a major role in sibling rivalry. Even parents' efforts to ease tensions between children can heighten competitiveness. This happens when a parent, perhaps without realizing it, sides with the sibling whose experience reflects the rivalries in that parent's own childhood. A parent who is an oldest child may favor an older sibling who feels displaced by a younger one. This can lead the younger child to feel left out.

Perhaps the most important aspect in which parents can prompt siblings to become rivals, however, is by comparing them to one another. Often parents, and even teachers and friends, challenge brothers and sisters to outdo one another without knowing it. Parents can place siblings at odds by saying things like "When your brother was your age he earned top grades, ran track, and had a part-time job. So there's no excuse for your failing marks." Such comments can make the younger sibling resent his or her brother. The

— 25

When parents compare siblings by pointing out the successes of one child to another, they can feed envy and resentment.

older brother did not do well to purposely hurt his younger sibling, but the effect may be the same.

Sister Rivalry:
Starving for Attention

Despite strides in the women's movement, sibling rivalry among sisters still often centers on comparisons of physical attractiveness. According to many, in our culture physical attractiveness and thinness are one. A mother or father who continually notes how attractive one daughter is over another may inspire sibling rivalry actually based on thinness.

Seeing it as a way to win parents' approval, many young girls pursue slimness at all costs. They may want to beat their sisters by being trimmer and will go to any lengths to do it. However, in some cases, it has cost them their health. At times, rivalry between sisters has led to serious eating disorders such as anorexia nervosa and bulimia. Anorexics starve themselves trying to be thin. Bulimics eat excessively and then may try to control their body weight by taking laxatives or forcing themselves to vomit.

According to Dr. Charles A. Murkofsky, director of the Eating Disorders Program at New York City's Gracie Square Hospital, "The problem begins with pressure to be thin and look good. . . . Then it becomes an endless issue with each [sister] asking herself, 'How thin am I compared to my sister?' "[1]

That's what happened to Michelle after her little sister, Ariel, started "turning into a real beauty," as their father put it. Michelle had clearly been her father's favorite when Ariel was small. He always said that he didn't enjoy babies and preferred being with an older child he could talk to. So while Michelle's mother cared for the baby,

— 27

Michelle and her father spent Saturday afternoons together at the library or going to the playground or to movies. Michelle loved those special times, and before long family, friends, and neighbors began calling her a "daddy's girl."

Michelle was an attractive child. But as Ariel grew older, people couldn't stop saying how unusually pretty she was. And by the time Ariel was in the second grade, everyone said that she should be an actress or model.

Ariel never had a weight problem. She ate whatever she liked without putting on a pound. Michelle noticed that her little sister didn't even seem to care for cake or candy. But Michelle loved sweets, and she knew that it showed.

Michelle's relationship with her father also began to change. She couldn't help but notice how proud her father seemed when someone complimented Ariel. It was also clear that he increasingly took Ariel's side when the girls argued.

Michelle felt that she was losing her father's affection, and she blamed Ariel for it. But the most painful blow came the day their father was to take both girls to a Saturday morning Christmas brunch at his office. Michelle planned to leave with her father and sister after an early-morning dental appointment. However, her appointment took longer than expected, and by the time she returned home Ariel and her father had already left.

Michelle was devastated. She felt that her father didn't care enough about her to have waited. As she put it: "Dad had my slender, beautiful sister to show off at the party, so I guess he didn't need me. I was only twenty minutes late. It wouldn't have killed them to wait for me."

When her father returned, he promised to take Michelle to next year's party. But the hurt she experienced that day did not quickly fade. Michelle became determined to win her father back. She didn't know if she'd ever be as pretty as Ariel, but she could make sure that she would be as thin. The next day Michelle began a strict diet. The more weight she lost, the closer she felt to her goal. Yet Michelle refused to stop dieting even after she was slimmer than her sister. Six months later she was diagnosed as having a severe case of anorexia nervosa and was hospitalized. After months of nutritional counseling and family therapy Michelle improved somewhat. However, before fully recovering, she had to explore her relationships with her sibling and parents.

Rivalry:
A Parent's Perspective

Some parents who foster competitiveness among their children may be unaware of doing so. When their households are rocked by feuding siblings, they often do not know how to defuse the situation. One mother described the fierce rivalry between her sons:

"My husband and I have two boys, two years apart in age. We love our sons equally and have always tried to treat them fairly, but unfortunately the boys don't see it that way. Whenever we praise one, the other acts as if we've insulted him. They fight over everything— who sits in the front seat of the car, who can swim more laps in the town pool, even who gets the larger piece of pie for dessert. Sometimes I think I need a slide rule to have a conflict-free dinner hour at our house.

"I'll never forget the first time I took my younger son, Brian, to the dentist. Both boys needed checkups, so they went together. Gary, my older son, felt at home at our dentist's office. The dentist was a family friend, and Gary had known him since he was small. When we arrived he jumped into the dentist's chair for his examination. But moments later we heard Brian crying in the waiting room.

— *29*

FOUR INCHES!

THREE AND SEVEN-EIGHTHS INCHES! I **KNEW** MINE WAS LESS! I WAS RIGHT! I WAS RIGHT! MOM LOVES YOU MORE!

Competition between brothers and sisters can reach some amazing— and amusing— extremes. Desserts and dentist chairs can become battlegrounds where children fight to see who's best and first.

— 30

"I felt bad for him. It was his first time at the dentist's, and I thought he must have been frightened. I tried to calm Brian, explaining that even though the dental equipment looked scary, the drill didn't hurt that much. I assured him that the dentist and nurse dressed in white were really nice people who were there to help him. I had begun to discuss the effects of decay on our teeth when Brian stopped crying. After catching his breath, he blurted out, 'I'm crying because I wanted to go first.' I couldn't believe my ears. My kids were even competing over seeing the dentist."

As suggested by this mother's story, most parents do not intentionally incite sibling rivalry. However, this isn't so for everyone. Sadly, a few parents may deliberately humiliate, betray, or physically punish their children for not measuring up to their brothers and sisters. Such parents are not only promoting rivalry, they are abusing their children and setting the stage for lifelong problems.

four

ONCE RIVALS, ALWAYS RIVALS?

Must sibling rivalry go hand in hand with having a brother or sister? Some experts seem to think so. According to psychologists Julius and Zelda Segal:

> *Rivalry is normal. Unfortunately, brothers and sisters often dwell together not in unity but in animosity. Their growing-up years are marked by constant bickering, teasing, and outright hostility. It should be consoling to know that a certain amount of rivalry between siblings is par for the course of childhood.* [1]

Adult Rivals

Sibling rivalry may be unavoidable, but isn't there hope that brothers and sisters will grow out of feeling jealous of and competitive with one another? As siblings become adults and lead their own lives, won't their diminished contact cause sibling rivalry to disappear?

— *33*

As adults, many siblings see less of each other. Old rivalries and envies, however, may still remain. No one expects siblings in their thirties, forties, or fifties to kick or bite one another. They may, however, express old rivalries in less obvious ways.

Jealousies may resurface at family gatherings such as weddings, christenings, funerals, and anniversary celebrations. A sibling may either boast about his own accomplishments or be overly critical of a brother or sister at a family party. For example, a man who over the years has kept in excellent physical shape may gloat about it to his heavier, flabbier brother. At holiday gatherings such as Thanksgiving dinners, an older sister might announce that her preschooler has just been admitted to an exclusive private nursery school. The news could hurt the woman's younger sister, who has been unsuccessfully trying to have a baby for five years. The older sister might even make things worse by asking if there is any good news yet.

Different Paths

Rivalry can, however, become less intense among siblings. For example, if one brother becomes a doctor and the other a lawyer, people are likely to say that each did well. But if both become doctors, the question of who has the more successful practice may continually come up.

At times, siblings who have been compared to a brother or sister throughout childhood may go out of their way to be different. One woman dealt with that situation in this way:

"By the time I was sixteen, I felt as though I'd spent a lifetime in my sister Cara's shadow. We didn't look all that different, but she was prettier. And even though I wasn't stupid, Cara always managed to do better in school. Our parents tried to be fair, but like everyone else they couldn't help but notice that things came more easily to Cara.

Brothers and sisters can avoid being rivals by choosing different career paths that won't lead to direct comparisons.

"I decided that part of the problem was that I'd purposely tried to follow in my sister's footsteps. I don't know why, it just always seemed natural to do whatever she did. But these were the things that Cara liked—so naturally she did better in them.

"At seventeen I finally felt ready to stop trying to be Cara and be myself. First I changed the way I looked. Cara always wore 'preppy-style' [conservative] outfits, and because she was thinner she looked better in them than I. I decided to find my own style. For a long time I had secretly liked clothes with a dramatic flair, so I used my baby-sitting money to buy two brightly colored capes, some unusual hats, and several big, chunky jewelry pieces.

"I think the most daring thing I did was change my hair. Cara and I both had light-brown hair that we wore fairly long. Without

— 35

ARE YOU TWINS ?

Beating the odds of being at odds can mean recognizing your uniqueness from your brother or sister—even when others don't.

telling anyone, I went to the beauty shop and had mine cut short and bleached blond. I thought our mother was going to pass out when she saw me, but she got used to it. After a while she even said she liked it. Best of all, people stopped saying how much Cara and I looked alike; instead they began to comment on how different we were.

"Yet perhaps the most important change came when I entered college. Both Cara and I were interested in psychology and creative writing, and Cara had become a psychology major. I began majoring in it as well, but found I liked my English classes better. So even though it took some courage to depart from the trail Cara blazed, I switched my major.

"It was the right choice. I had done well as a psychology major, but never as well as Cara. Yet in English my grade average was even sometimes better than hers. Although we were both still students, I felt the competition between us decrease. At last Cara was free to do well in psychology without worrying about her little sister gaining on her. And I no longer felt bad about getting a B in a course where Cara got an A. It's funny because we both still like psychology and English.

"Now that we're out of school things are even better. Cara is a successful psychologist. However, her writing ability enables her to produce outstanding research papers. I've become a fairly well-known author. Yet some of my best-selling novels are psychological thrillers. My relationship with my sister couldn't be more rewarding. We have stopped trying to outdo each other and are good friends."

Learning to
Deal with Rivalry

Dealing with sibling rivalry is a worthwhile goal for any brother or sister—and you don't have to wait until you are adults to begin. These are some ways to ease the tensions of sibling rivalry:

- Remember that everyone is special in his or her own way. Your strengths may differ from those of your sibling, but they are just as valuable. So if a sibling does well in a particular area, be proud of him or her. That person is merely different from—not better than—you.

- Look at sibling rivalry as a way for you to become more "you." Psychologist Barry Ginsberg believes that sibling rivalry can motivate people to establish their own identities as well as take part in society. Siblings, he says, not only "have to learn to live with others . . . [but] they've got to find a space of their own and develop a sense of personal autonomy [or sense of independence]."[2]

- Realize that sibling rivalry sometimes can propel people to greater heights. Consider the case of television actress Joanna Kerns and her sister Donna de Varona. Donna, the older sister, was an Olympic gold-medal swimmer. Hoping to do as well as her sister, Joanna took up gymnastics. However, she fell short of her goal. Not only did she fail to make the Olympic team, but a permanent knee injury dashed her hopes of a future as an athlete.

  Yet with her sister's reputation to live up to, Joanna felt she couldn't give up on being successful. Instead of gymnastics, however, she poured her energy into acting and eventually became famous. Joanna credits her success to sibling competitiveness. "I never would have gotten out of Santa Clara [her home town] if it wasn't for my sister Donna," the star confesses.

Sibling rivalry can also be beneficial in other ways. By working out sibling conflicts, young people can learn how to better relate to others outside the home. After the yelling stops and the dust settles, most siblings try to compromise and cooperate. And these skills are crucial for later business and personal relationships.

Friends for Life

Siblings can be rivals for life, but they can also be much more. Siblings can provide needed support when a parent is either too busy or too annoyed to be there for you. There is also power in numbers. Brothers and sisters often band together to present a united front if they think their parents have been unfair.

Overcoming sibling rivalry can give a family's children a sense of strength through unity.

Because of sibling rivalry, brothers and sisters take a lot of hard knocks from each other. But if they learn to work things out, they can find that siblings are among their best . . .

40

A sibling also can be a lifelong friend. That's because brothers and sisters have so much in common. The biological or blood tie between them makes their bond special. "Only about three percent of [adult] siblings ever disconnect their relationship with one another permanently,"[3] notes psychology professor Dr. Michael Kahn.

Friends and co-workers may move away or change jobs, romances and marriages do not always last, but our brothers and sisters are always our brothers and sisters. As Dr. Kahn says: "In the stressful, fast-paced world we live in, the sibling relationship becomes for many the only intimate connection that seems to last."[4]

Rivalry among brothers and sisters can sometimes be hurtful and unsettling. But if they learn to deal with jealousy and competition, siblings can have relationships with one another that are among the most permanent and rewarding in life.

. . . and closest friends.

— *41*

endnotes

Chapter One

    1. Nancy Rubin, "Kids' Fights," *Parents* 63 (March 1988), p. 98.

Chapter Two

    1. Kim Wright Wiley, "My Sister, Myself," *Health* 20 (April 1988), p. 47.

Chapter Three

    1. Kim Wright Wiley, "My Sister, Myself," *Health* 20 (April 1988), p. 84.

Chapter Four

    1. Julius and Zelda Segal, "Siblings—Friends or Foes?" *Parents* 63 (November 1988), p. 250.
    2. Nancy Rubin, "Kids' Fights," *Parents* 63 (March 1988), p. 97.
    3. Dan Morris, "Mom Liked You Best; How Christians Outgrow Sibling Rivalry," *U.S. Catholic* 54 (January 1989), p. 6.
    4. Elizabeth Stark, "Beyond Rivalry," *Psychology Today* 22 (April 1988), p. 61.

further reading

Nonfiction

Cole, Joanna. *The New Baby at Your House*. New York: Morrow, 1985.
Hodder, Elizabeth. *Stepfamilies*. New York: Gloucester, 1990.
Jenness, Aylette. *Families: A Celebration of Diversity, Commitment and Love*. Boston: Houghton Mifflin, 1989.
Krementz, Jill. *How It Feels When Your Parents Divorce*. New York: Knopf, 1984.
LeShan, Eda J. *Grandparents: A Special Kind of Love*. New York: Macmillan, 1984.
——. *When Grownups Drive You Crazy*. New York: Macmillan, 1988.
Rosenberg, Maxine. *Brothers and Sisters*. New York: Clarion Books, 1991.
——. *Talking About Stepfamilies*. New York: Bradbury Press, 1990.

Fiction

Hamilton, Morse. *Little Sisters for Sale*. New York: Cobblehill, 1992.
Lakin, Patricia. *Don't Touch My Room*. Boston: Little, Brown, 1985.
Pevsner, Stella. *And You Give Me a Pain, Elaine*. Boston: Houghton Mifflin, 1978.
Sachs, Marilyn. *What My Sister Remembered*. New York: Dutton, 1992.
Simon, Nora. *How Do I Feel?* Morton Grove, Ill.: Whitman, 1970.

index

Adult sibling rivalry, 12, 33–34
Age differences, 14–15
Anger, 19
Anorexia nervosa, 27, 29
Autonomy, 38

Bedroom sharing, 15
Blended families, 21–22, 24
Bulimia, 27

Career paths, 34–35, 37
Chores, 17, 19
Comparisons, 17, 18, 25–28
Competitiveness, 12, 14–15, 17, 25, 41
Compromise, 38
Contact, 14–16
Cooperation, 38

de Varona, Donna, 38

Divorce, 19–21

Eating disorders, 27, 29
Emotional distance, 14–15
Emotional illness, 12

Family planning, 16
Family size, 16–17
Family therapy, 29
Farber, Sharon, 12
Fear, 19
Financial concerns, 16, 24
Firstborns, 12
Friendship, 15, 39, 41

Gender, 18–19
Ginsberg, Barry, 38
Grandparents, 24
Guilt, 19

Hand-me-down clothes, 15
Holiday gatherings, 34

Immigrant families, 16
Independence, 38

Jealousies, 12, 17, 34, 41

Kahn, Michael, 41
Kerns, Joanna, 38

Math, 19
Murkofsky, Charles A., 27

New baby, 8, 10, 12
Nutritional counseling, 29

Physical appearance, 27
Physical differences, 19
Physical illness, 12

Responsibilities, siblings as, 17

Sadness, 19
Same-sex siblings, 18–19, 27–29, 34–35, 37, 38
Science, 19
Segal, Julius, 33

Segal, Zelda, 33
Sibling rivalry
    adult, 12, 33–34
    age differences, 14–15
    comparisons and, 17, 18, 25–28
    contact and, 14–16
    dealing with, 37–38
    different career paths, 34–35, 37
    divorce, 19–21
    family size and, 16–17
    gender and, 18–19
    parent's perspective, 25, 29, 31, 32
    sisters, 9–11, 18–19, 27–29, 34–35, 37, 38
    step-families, 21–24
Sibling support, 16
Sisters, 9–11, 18–19, 27–29, 34–35, 37, 38
Social stereotypes, 19
Spacing children, 9
Sports, 15
Step-families, 21–24

Talents, 17
Thinness, 27

Women's movement, 27
Working mothers, 16